The Experiment Game

Book Six of
The Gift of Numbers
Math Fantasy Curriculum

Rachel Rogers and Joe Lineberry

Illustrations by ARTE RAVE

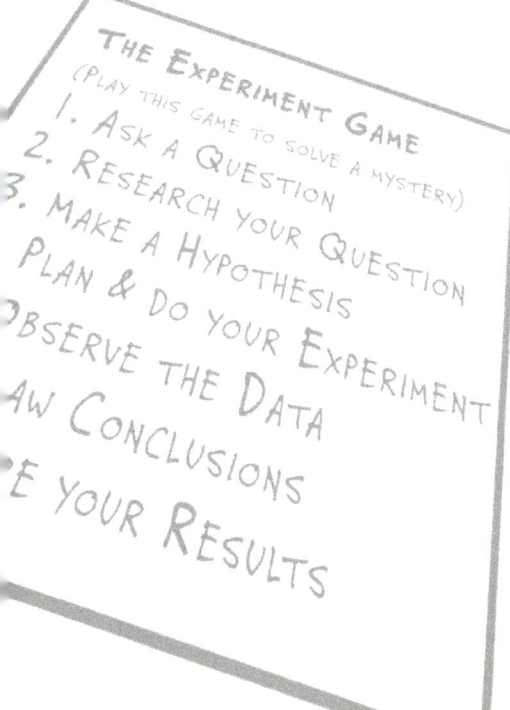

an imprint of
PROSPECTIVE PRESS LLC
1959 Peace Haven Rd, #246, Winston-Salem, NC 27106 U.S.A.
www.prospectivepress.com

Published in the United States of America by PROSPECTIVE PRESS LLC

THE EXPERIMENT GAME

Text copyright © Rachel Rogers and Joe Lineberry, 2021
All rights reserved.
The authors' moral rights have been asserted.

Illustrations by ARTE RAVE
© Prospective Press, 2021
All rights reserved.
The illustrator's moral rights have been asserted.

ISBN 978-1-943419-12-8

ProP-G008

The Experiment Game is the sixth volume in the Gift of Numbers math fantasy curriculum. For information on additional volumes in the series or for bulk sales, please send inquiries to education@prospectivepress.com

Printed in the United States of America
First softcover printing November, 2021

The text of this book is typeset in Mouse Memoirs
Accent text is typeset in Galindo

PUBLISHER'S NOTE

This book is a work of creative non-fiction with fictional fantasy elements. The people, names, characters, locations, activities, and events portrayed or implied by this book are the product of the author's imagination or are used fictitiously. Any resemblance to actual people, locations, and events is strictly coincidental. No actual kings were harmed during the writing of this book.

Without limiting the rights as reserved in the above copyright, no part of this publication may be reproduced, stored in or introduced into any retrieval system, or transmitted–by any means, in any form, electronic, mechanical, photocopying, recording, or otherwise–without the prior written permission of the publisher. Not only is such reproduction illegal and punishable by law, but it also hurts the authors and illustrator who toiled hard on the creation of this work and the publisher who brought it to the world. In the spirit of fair play, and to honor the labor and creativity of the authors and illustrator, we ask that you purchase only authorized electronic and print editions of this work and refrain from participating in or encouraging piracy or electronic piracy of copyright-protected materials. Please give creators a break and don't steal this or any other work.

Dedicated to our committed teachers, who care so much for our children.

"Detective Science was looking for clues on the football field. "What caused so many football players to disappear?" he wondered.

He joined Coach Winner and King Less. The king quietly said, "I had the odd number football team drink the magic formula from Dream Princess. You know, the sugary mixture that keeps numbers from disappearing."

"They drank some each day. But the magic formula didn't work, did it?" said Coach Winner. "We had six odd number football players vanish. Six even number football players also disappeared.

"I was worried about our team playing well. That sugary magic formula caused our team to run more slowly each day. I think our team would have been too slow to win the game."

"Coach Winner leaned over to the detective. "Did you notice?" asked the coach. "No football fans vanished, while twelve football players disappeared. What did the players do differently than the fans?"

"Good question," replied Detective Science. "Let's talk more in my office tomorrow morning. We can discuss my new discovery. It is called the experiment game. Maybe it will help us solve our mystery of the missing numbers."

King More, King Less, and Doctor Even jogged to work the next day. They were waiting outside Detective Science's office. King More leaned over to King Less, "I'm looking forward to hearing about the experiment game."

"I have an idea about this game," said King More. "I guess the experiment game will include many long words. You know, the detective likes to use long words."

Detective Science arrived and led them into his office. On his wall were the rules for his new experiment game. King More was right. The detective had used several long words.

The Experiment Game
(Play this game to solve a mystery)
1. Ask a Question
2. Research your Question
3. Make a Hypothesis
4. Plan & do your Experiment
5. Observe the Data
6. Draw Conclusions
7. Share your Results

Detective Science was trembling with excitement. "Look at my new game!" he exclaimed. "I think this will help us solve the mystery of the missing numbers."

"The **experiment** game will help future boys and girls, too. They will use this game to solve their mysteries. When they do science experiments, they will learn new information on their own."

> Our question:
> - What is causing our numbers to disappear?

"How do we play this game?" asked King More.

"Let's start with Step 1. Ask yourself a question about something you don't understand," said the detective.

"I have a question," blurted King Less. "What is causing our numbers to disappear?"

"I agree," replied Detective Science. "That question is the mystery we are trying to solve. Let me write that down so we don't forget it. The second step is to **research** your question. That means to read information about your topic and talk to others about what they have seen or learned related to your topic."

What Time of Day Did Numbers Disappear?

Morning Operations	😔
Afternoon Operations	😔 😔 😔 😔 😔 😔 😔

When Did Numbers Start Disappearing?

Before Zero Arrived	
After Zero Arrived	😔 😔 😔 😔 😔 😔 😔 😔

Key
Each 😔 = 2 Numbers Who Disappeared

"Remember we have already done some research," continued the detective. "We made some pictographs about when the numbers were disappearing. The first graph shows more numbers disappeared in the afternoon."

"The second pictograph shows that all the numbers disappeared after ghostly zero showed up," observed King Less.

RESEARCH

- ONLY FOOTBALL PLAYERS DISAPPEARED
- ONLY FOOTBALL PLAYERS DRANK MOUNTAIN WATER

"You are correct again, King Less," said the detective. "In my research after the game, I also found only football players disappeared. No fans disappeared at the game."

King More added, "The local grocery store gave all its mountain water to the football teams. No bottles of mountain water were available to sell to the fans. Only football players drank mountain water that day."

"Wow!" said Doctor Even. "I just thought of another fact. We always serve mountain water at the hospital with our afternoon snacks. We serve apple juice during the morning operations, but we serve mountain water in the afternoon."

The group reviewed the research on the board. The detective spoke first, "I believe we are at Step 3. We may have a **hypothesis**."

"Wait a minute. That's a long word," said King More. "What does 'hypothesis' mean?"

"A hypothesis is a guess based on facts," answered Detective Science. "I think our hypothesis is 'Drinking mountain water causes numbers to disappear.' Based on our research, that seems like a good guess."

The Experiment Game
(Play this game to solve a mystery)
1. Ask a Question
2. Research your Question
3. Make a (Hypothesis) — *a guess based on facts.*
4. Plan & Do your Experiment
5. Observe the Data
6. Draw Conclusions
7. Share your Results

Our hypothesis:
- Drinking mountain water causes numbers to disappear.

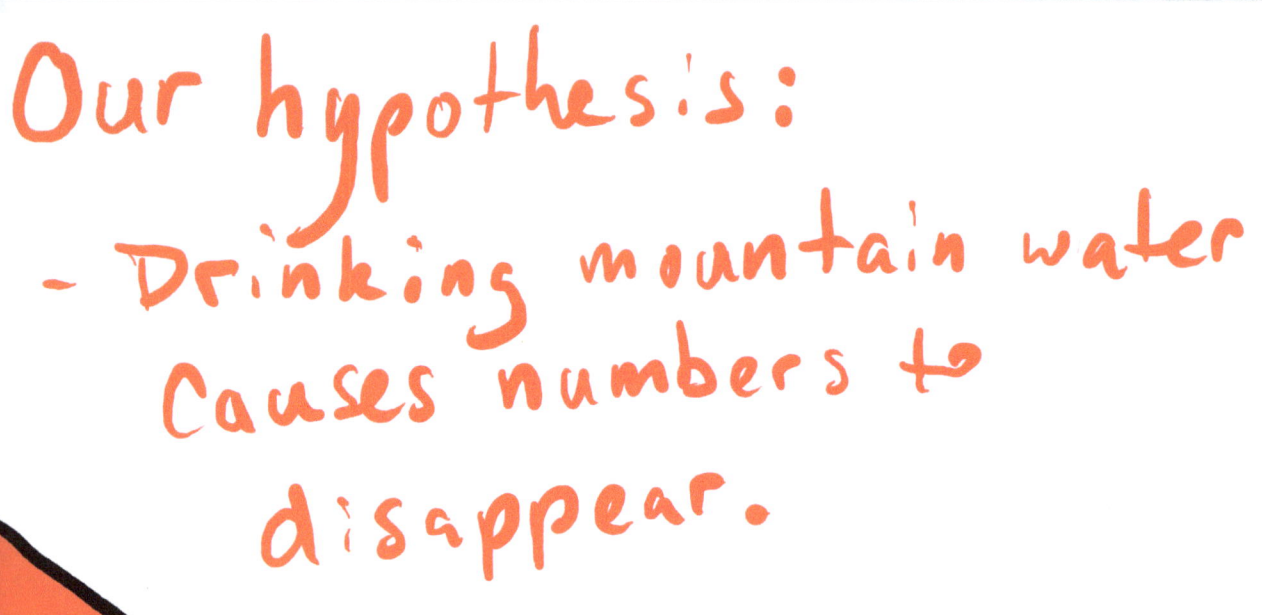

"Oh no!" cried King Less. "I drank three bottles of mountain water..."

Poof!

King Less vanished. His crown rattled to the floor.

"Hurry!" yelled Doctor Even. "We need to form a quick fact family to bring King Less back. Which of our numbers can we use to make a 1? I'm an 8, King More is a 2, and Detective Science is a 7."

$$8 - 7 = 1$$

They figured it out quickly. They subtracted seven from eight to get one.

King Less reappeared.

After he recovered, he moaned, "That proves it. I disappeared after drinking mountain water, so mountain water must be causing our numbers to disappear."

"No," said Detective Science to King Less. "That may be true, or it may not be true. We need to move to Step 4—Plan and Do Your Experiment. Our experiment will try to prove whether drinking mountain water causes numbers to vanish."

"Wait!" said Doctor Even. "'Experiment' is another long word. I know we are playing the experiment game, but what is an experiment?"

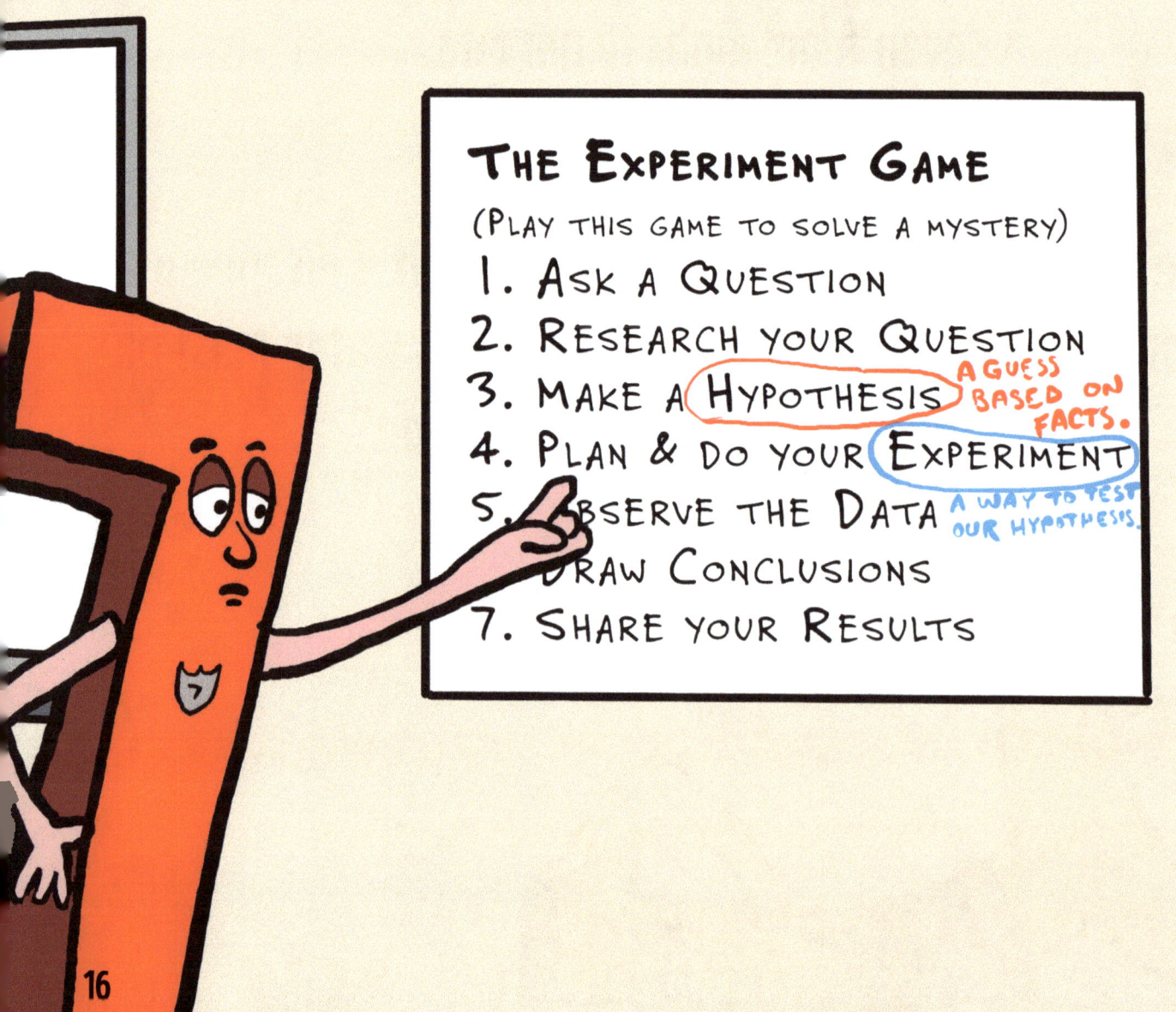

THE EXPERIMENT GAME
(PLAY THIS GAME TO SOLVE A MYSTERY)
1. ASK A QUESTION
2. RESEARCH YOUR QUESTION
3. MAKE A HYPOTHESIS — A GUESS BASED ON FACTS.
4. PLAN & DO YOUR EXPERIMENT — A WAY TO TEST OUR HYPOTHESIS.
5. OBSERVE THE DATA
6. DRAW CONCLUSIONS
7. SHARE YOUR RESULTS

King More jumped into the conversation, "I know. I know. Detective Science told me the definition yesterday. An **experiment** is a way to test our hypothesis. An experiment can help us prove if mountain water is causing our numbers to disappear."

"Good memory," said Detective Science. "It may help us solve this mystery. We do need a way to test our hypothesis."

RESEARCH

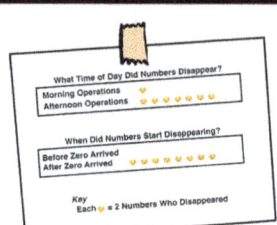

* PLAN AND DO YOUR EXPERIMENT *

"We need to set up our experiment correctly," continued Detective Science. "We need two groups. Group 1 will drink one bottle of mountain water at their morning and afternoon breaks. Group 2 will drink one bottle of regular water when they take their breaks."

The detective added, "We also need to make sure all other **characteristics** of both groups are the same."

King Less was feeling better. He had been listening well. "'Characteristics' is another long word. Are you trying to say that everything else about the groups needs to be the same?"

"Yes, " replied the detective. "Let me explain how our experiment could work. That might help you understand what I mean."

Experiment Venn Diagram

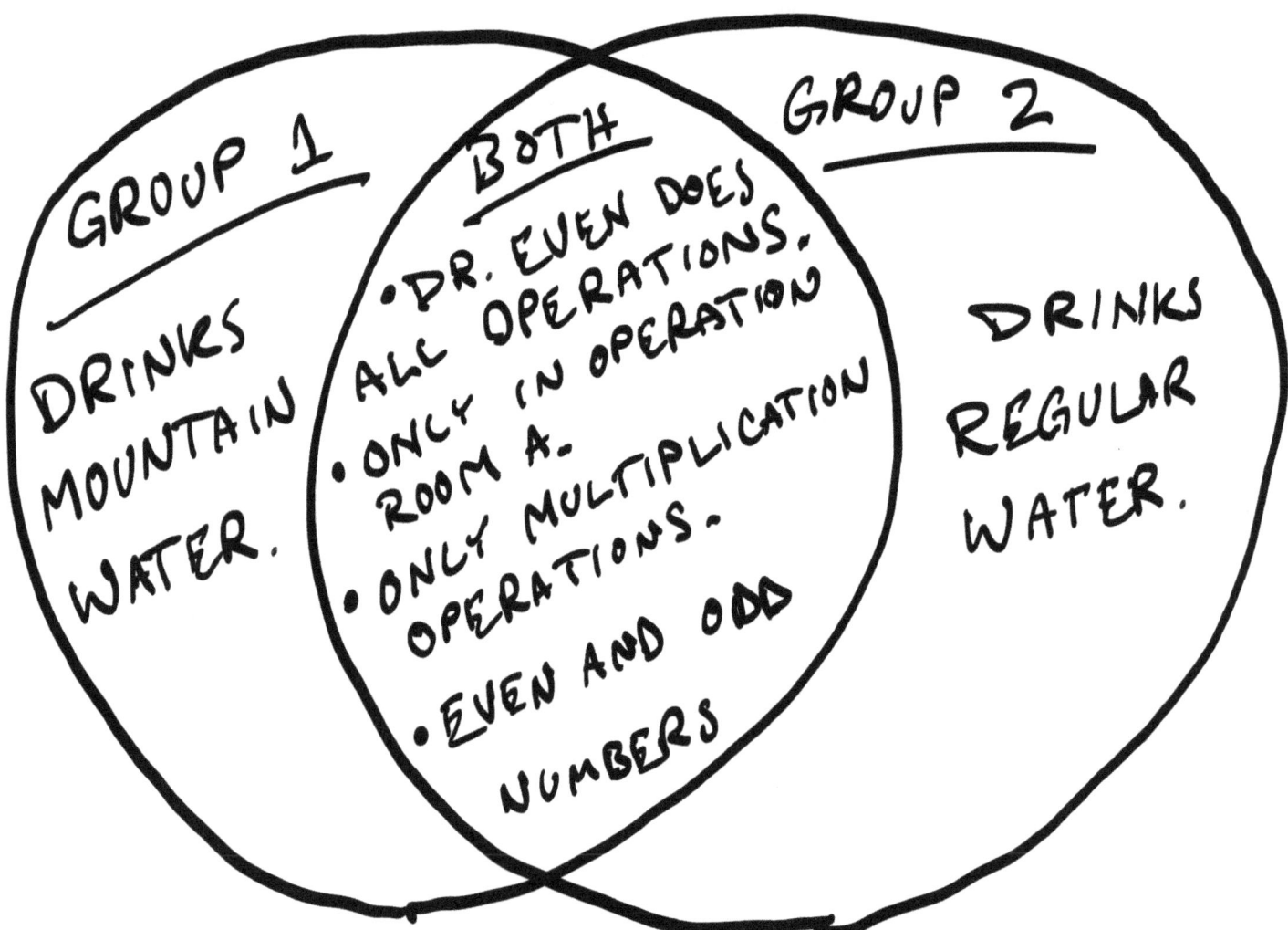

"We can have Doctor Even perform the experiment. He will do math operations only in Operation Room A, and he will only do multiplication operations. We will use an equal number of odd and even numbers in each group."

"We want drinking mountain water to be the only difference in the two groups. Everything else will be the same in the two groups."

"Let's do it!" said King More. "We have our plan. I will take care of Step 5—Observe the **Data**. I have my note pad ready. I will write down the data—the information we learn about how many numbers disappear from each group."

"I'm excited," said the detective. "Let's meet in my office in a week with the data you recorded. Maybe these results will help us solve our mystery."

"During the next week Doctor Even conducted the experiment each day. Doctor Odd made sure Group 1 only drank mountain water during their snack breaks. Group 2 only drank regular water during their snack breaks.

King More wrote down the count of numbers who disappeared from each group. King Less made sure that the fact families were there to restore the numbers when they disappeared.

It was a team effort.

At the end of the week King More and Doctor Even made a chart and a graph of the data from their experiment. They showed it to Detective Science, King Less, and Doctor Odd.

	Count of Numbers Who Disappeared					
	Monday	Tuesday	Wednesday	Thursday	Friday	Total
Group 1--The Numbers Who Drank Mountain Water	2	4	3	2	2	13
Group 2--The Numbers Who Drank Regular Water	0	1	0	0	0	1

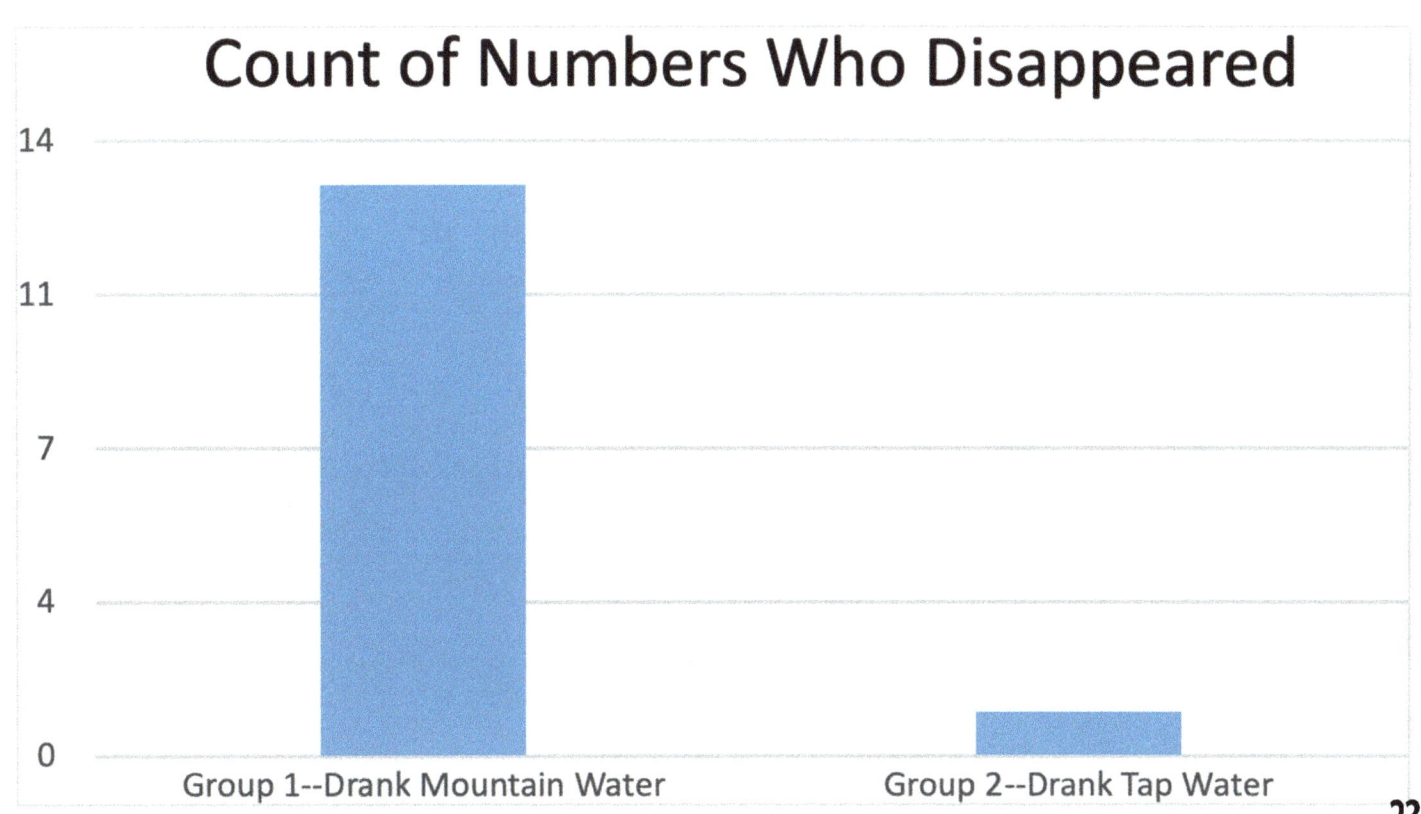

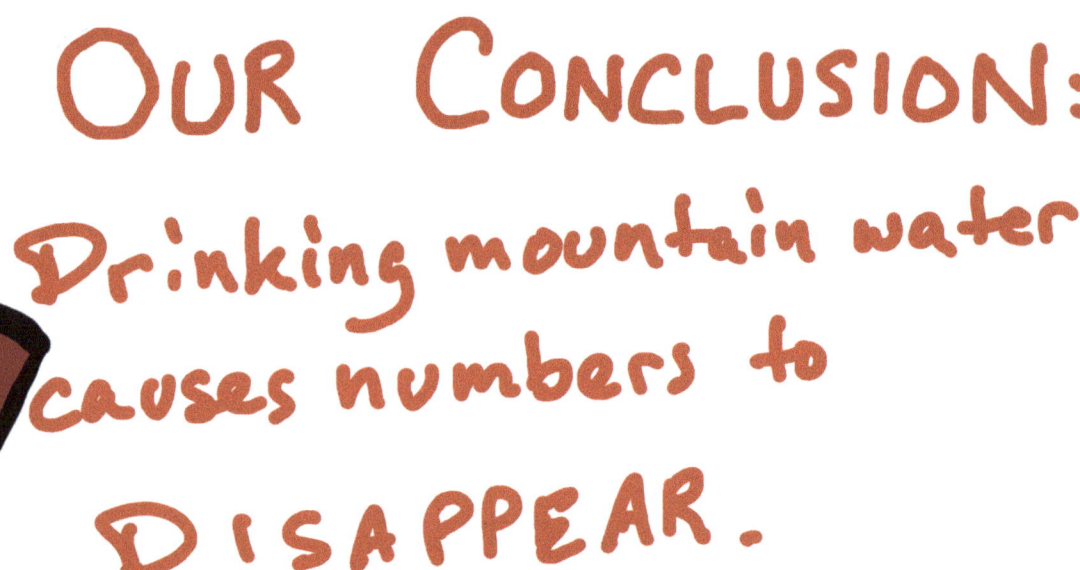

"I think we can move to Step 6—Draw Conclusions," said the detective. "Look at these results—13 numbers who drank mountain water disappeared. Only 1 number who drank regular water disappeared."

"We can conclude that drinking mountain water is a big cause of our numbers disappearing."

King More and Doctor Even worked together to complete Step 7—Share your Results. Doctor Even first wrote the abstract:

Abstract

Purpose: What is causing numbers to disappear?

Hypothesis: Drinking mountain water causes numbers to disappear.

Procedure: Doctor Even performed multiplication operations for one week in Operation A. Numbers were put into two groups during the operations. Group 1 drank one bottle of mounttan water during their snack breaks, and Group 2 drank one bottle of regular water during their snack breaks.

Conclusion: 13 numbers in Group 1 disappeared and 1 number in Group 2 disappeared. We conclude that drinking mountain water causes numbers to disappear.

King More worked on the **triptych** display board.

Purpose
What is causing numbers to disappear?

Hypothesis
Drinking mountain water causes numbers to disappear

Research
More numbers disppeared in afternoon operations;
All numbers disppeared after zero appeared;
Twelve football players disappeared after drinking mountain water.

The Mystery of the Missi

Materials & Procedu
Operations were performed for on

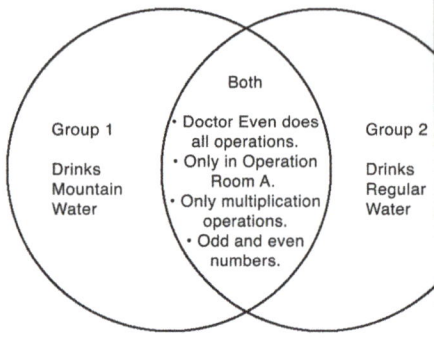

Group 1
Drinks Mountain Water

Both
- Doctor Even does all operations.
- Only in Operation Room A.
- Only multiplication operations.
- Odd and even numbers.

Group 2
Drinks Regular Water

Data

	Monday
Group 1--The Numbers Who Drank Mountain Water	9
Group 2--The Numbers Who Drank Regular Water	9

It was the perfect way to share the results with Detective Science and the others.

Everyone was excited. They now knew that mountain water caused most of the numbers to disappear. If numbers stopped drinking mountain water, they should stop most numbers from vanishing.

King More announced, "In honor of Detective Science, his successful game, and his love for long words, I officially change the name of the experiment game to the scientific method."

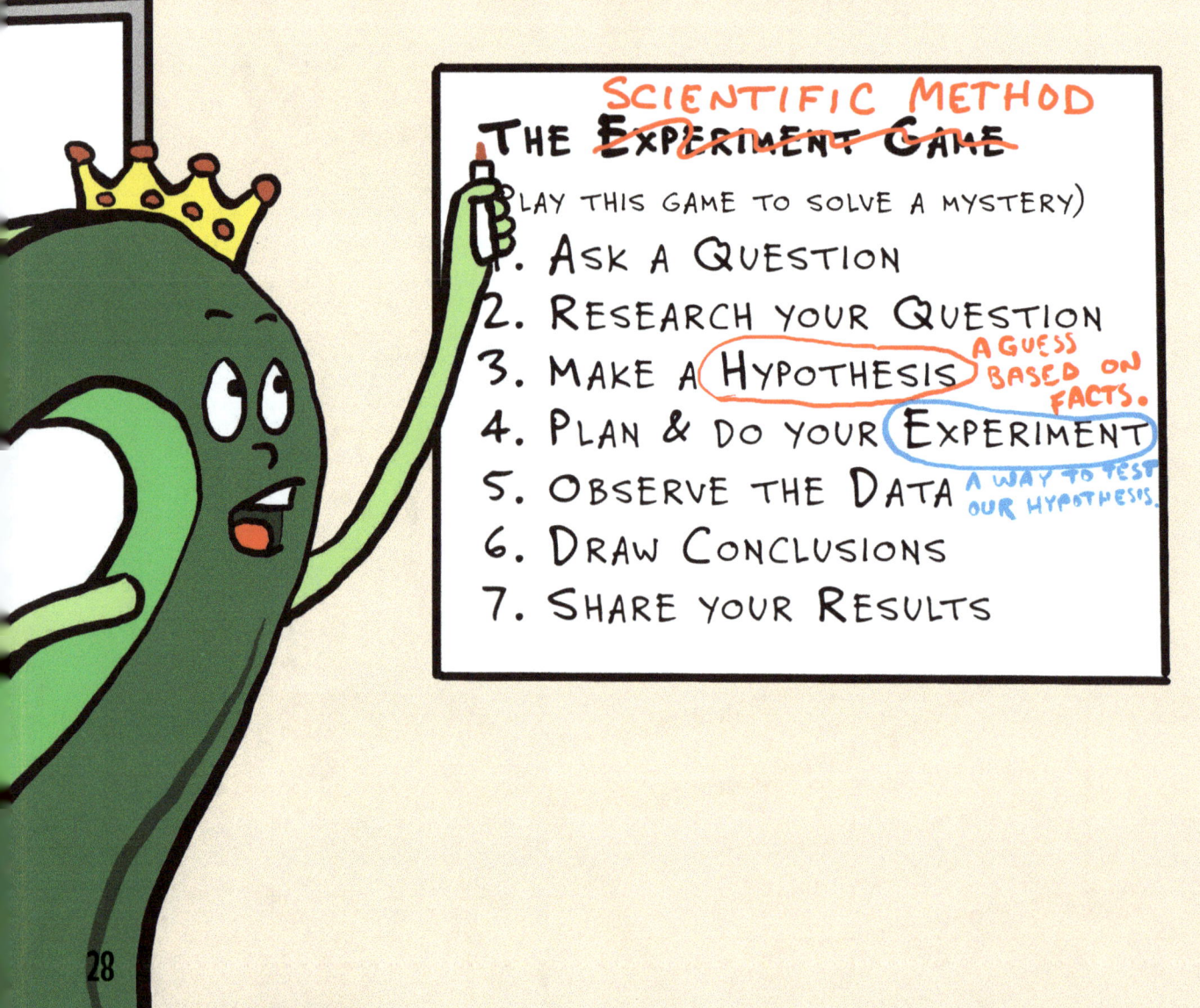

They all cheered for Detective Science. King More added, "Let's celebrate with a fruit smoothie party."

Detective Science was happy. He was also curious. He was talking to himself. King Less heard him mumble, "I wonder what is in mountain water that causes numbers to disappear."

"We need to go see Dream Princess," King Less told the detective. "They bottle mountain water from the river near her store. I also need to see her to get a refund on her magic formula. It didn't keep my odd number football players from disappearing."

The two friends agreed to go see the princess . . . but only after they drank smoothies with their friends.

The Experiment Game Exercise

Let's pretend the experiment in *The Experiment Game* had different results. What if the results had been:

	Count of Numbers Who Disappeared					
	Monday	Tuesday	Wednesday	Thursday	Friday	Total
Group 1--The Numbers Who Drank Mountain Water	2	1	3	1	1	8
Group 2--The Numbers Who Drank Regular Water	1	1	2	3	1	8

Look at the abstract on page 25. What parts of the abstract would stay the same with these results? What parts of the abstract would change? How would you change the wording of the abstract?

Now it is your turn to solve a mystery by doing your own experiment. You get to play the experiment game.

1. Ask a Question—What mystery do you want to solve?

2. Research your Question—Read what others have written about your question. Ask others about your question.

3. Make a Hypothesis—What is your educated guess about the answer to your question?

4. Plan and do your Experiment—What steps will you take to test your hypothesis?

5. Observe the Data—Record the information about the results of your experiment.

6. Draw Conclusions—Do the results show your hypothesis was true?

7. Share your Results—Write your abstract and display your results on your triptych.

The Publisher hereby grants permission to the original purchaser and/or sole owner of this book to make copies of this page for in-class use only. Copies may not be transmitted, sold, lent, or stored–electronically or otherwise.

Discussion Questions

1. If you could design *The Experiment Game* as a game for sale at the toy store, what would the game look like? Would you play the game on a board or on your computer or on your television?

2. To honor Detective Science, King Less renamed the experiment game. The new name is the _____ method. It is a way to _____.

3. What are the seven steps of the experiment game? Which step is your favorite step? Why is it your favorite step?

4. Define "hypothesis." Define "data." Why is each of these words important when conducting an experiment?

5. Why did the authors write The Experiment Game?

The Publisher hereby grants permission to the original purchaser and/or sole owner of this book to make copies of this page for in-class use only. Copies may not be transmitted, sold, lent, or stored—electronically or otherwise.

Glossary

Abstract — short version of a science fair project final report. The abstract is shown at the beginning of the final report and it can be shown on the display board (triptych). Usually about 250 words.

Characteristic — a specific feature that describes a person or a group.

Data — information that is collected about a topic.

Experiment — a scientific test that is conducted to test a hypothesis.

Glossary — an alphabetical list of hard or unusual words relating to a topic or subject. Each word is defined (meaning given) and found in the back of the book.

Hypothesis — a prediction or idea of what you think will happen in an experiment; a guess based on your research.

Research — to read and study information in order to discover new facts about a topic.

Triptych — a board divided into three parts that are designed to be displayed together. Science Fair triptychs are cardboard made to stand up.

About the Authors

Rachel Rogers
retired from Old Richmond Elementary School, Winston-Salem, NC, after more than 42 years of teaching first, second, and third graders.

Joe Lineberry
told similar stories to his sons when they were growing up. He is also the author of *Let's Stop Playing Games: Finding Freedom in Authentic Living.*

About the Books

The Gift of Numbers
is a math fantasy curriculum that combines literature and mathmatics in a fun, age-appropriate series for second- and third-grade students.

- Volume 1: *Saved by Addition*
- Volume 2: *Surprised by Subtraction*
- Volume 3: *Graphing the Mystery*
- Volume 4: *Adventure with Fractions*
- Volume 5: *Multiplication Football*
- Volume 6: *The Experiment Game*
- Volume 7: *Division Gymnastics*

www.ingramcontent.com/pod-product-compliance
Lightning Source LLC
Chambersburg PA
CBHW051355110526
44592CB00024B/2990